Written by
Lindi Masters

Illustrated by
Lizzie Masters

REALMS OF THE KINGDOM, MOUNTAINS AND THE THRONE OF GRACE

Published by

Written by©
Lindi Masters

Illustrated by©
Lizzie Masters

"REALMS OF THE KINGDOM, MOUNTAINS AND THE THRONE OF GRACE"
Copyright© 2018

Story written by Lindi Masters
Illustrated and Designed by Lizzie Masters

Thank you to IGNITE KIDZHUB© and all the kids from the UK, USA, South Africa and Australia for their artwork.
Special thanks to our mentors and friends Ian Clayton and Grant Mahoney, without whom we wouldn't have explored these realms.

This edition published by Seraph Creative in 2018©
www.seraphcreative.org

All rights reserved.© No part of this publication may be reproduced, stored in a retrieval system or transmitted, in any form or by any means, electronic, mechanical, photocopying, recording or otherwise, without the prior permission of the copyright holder.

ISBN 978-0-6399841-0-0

All rights reserved.© No part of this book, artwork included may be used or reproduced in any manner without the written permission of the publisher.

This book belongs to:

_____

REALMS OF THE KINGDOM

- ETERNITY
- PERFECTION
- HEAVEN OF HEAVENS
- HEAVEN
- KINGDOM OF HEAVEN
- KINGDOM OF GOD
- KINGDOM OF THE EARTH

Heaven is a wonderful place.

It is in another dimension and is available for you to visit anytime you want to.

Heaven has many dimensions.
It is not only one place.
John 14:2 says, 'In my father's heart are many dimensions'.

KINGDOM OF THE EARTH

The Kingdom of the Earth is where we find the mobile court.

This is where the accuser accuses us.

This is where we get forgiveness and scrolls and the accuser ha-satan is judged.

1 John 1:9

KINGDOM OF GOD

We enter into the Kingdom of God through the veil of YHVH יהוה and His blood.

This is the new and living way.

In the atomsphere of Heaven is the realm of His government.

Hebrews 10:19-20

KINGDOM OF HEAVEN

In the Kingdom of Heaven we find the realms of dominion.

Dominion means where we can command, have power and rule as Lords.

HEAVEN

This is the realm where Yahweh, YHVH lives, this is where you operate as a King.

We find the Outer Court, the Inner Court and the Holy of Holies in this realm.

HEAVEN OF HEAVENS

This is where we can operate as a king of kings. This is the place of His dominion.

When you are in charge of something or rule it, you have dominion over it.

PERFECTION AND ETERNITY

Perfection is the place of His government, this is the court where the 70 chancellors sit and govern.

Eternity is the place of His presence.

MOUNTAINS

We all have mountains that Yeshua has given us.

Mountains always show a place of government in our lives.

If there are dragons on your mountains you can kill them with the sword of the spirit.

You can sit on the mountain of your life and rule and reign.

1 Peter 2:9
'But you are God's chosen treasure. Priests who are Kings'.

Let's practice...

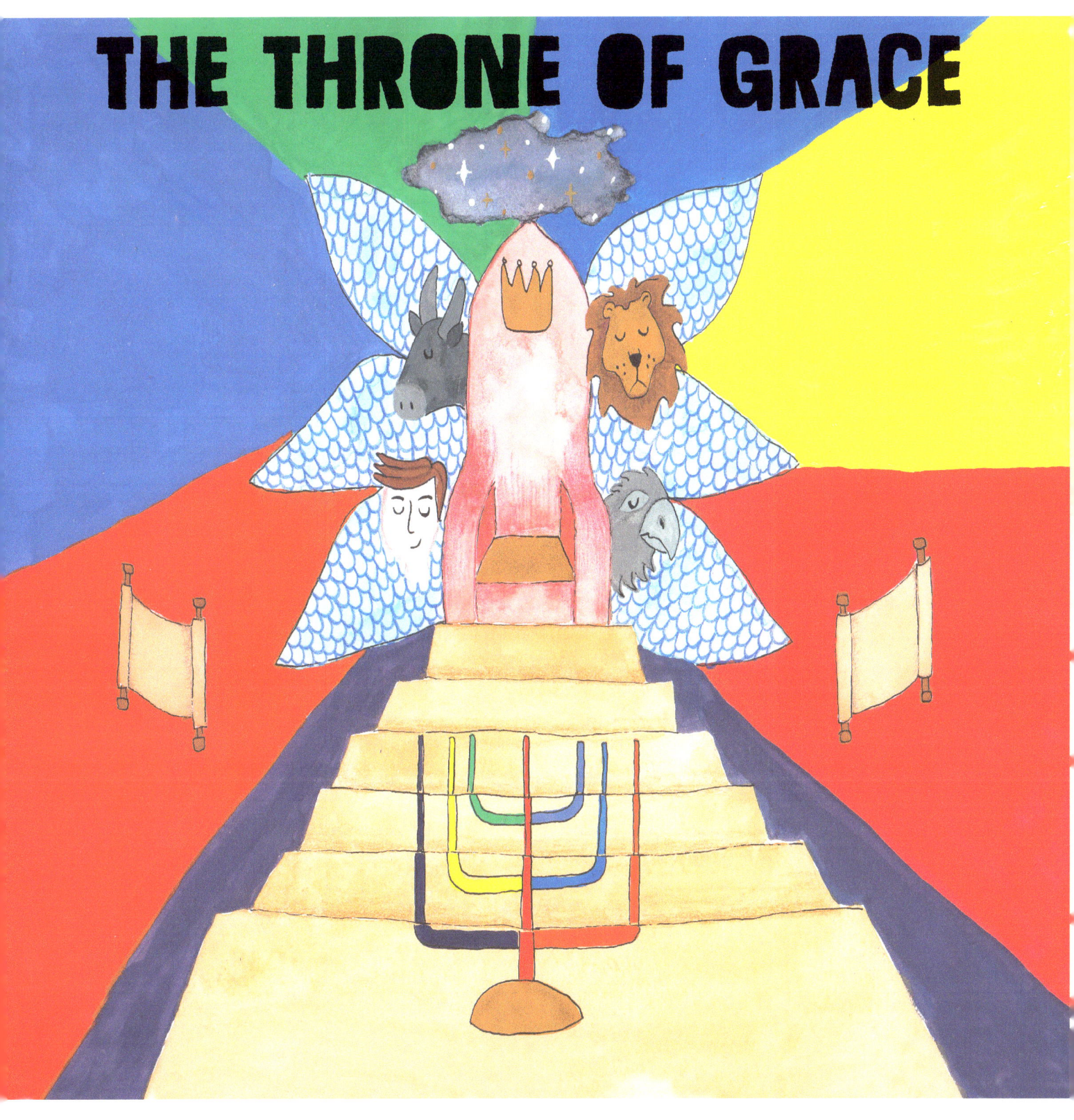

The Throne of Grace is not where the mobile court is.

This is a place where anyone can receive His mercy and find grace. And God gives us help and mercy when we need it.

Enter through the veil of His flesh into the Throne of Grace.

Come to His Throne and say, 'please give me Grace and Mercy to help me because I have a need'.

This is an exciting place where Holy Spirit brings you into the dimension of Yahweh whenever you need to.

AMEN!

Fighting dragons on my mountain. Hannah- South Africa

Around the Throne of God.
Carla- Australia

The twenty-four elders fall down before Him who sits on the throne and worship Him who lives forever and ever, and cast their crowns before the throne.
Revelations 4:10

Mountains.
Anne Marie- USA

God's Throne.
Jeiel- UK

Out of my heart shall flow rivers of living water

John 7:38

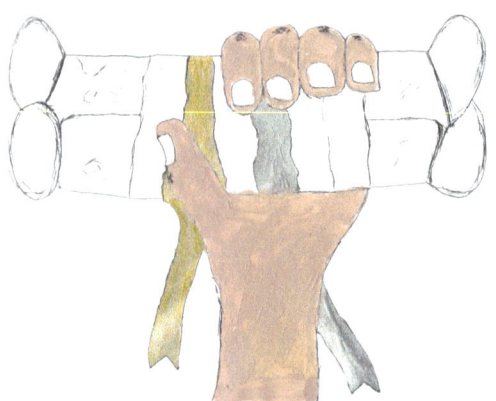
Scroll of my life.
Joel- South Africa

Throne of Grace.
Hendriette- UK

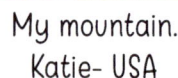
My mountain.
Katie- USA

Realms of the Kingdom.
Luke- Australia

Realms of the Kingdom.
Reuel- UK

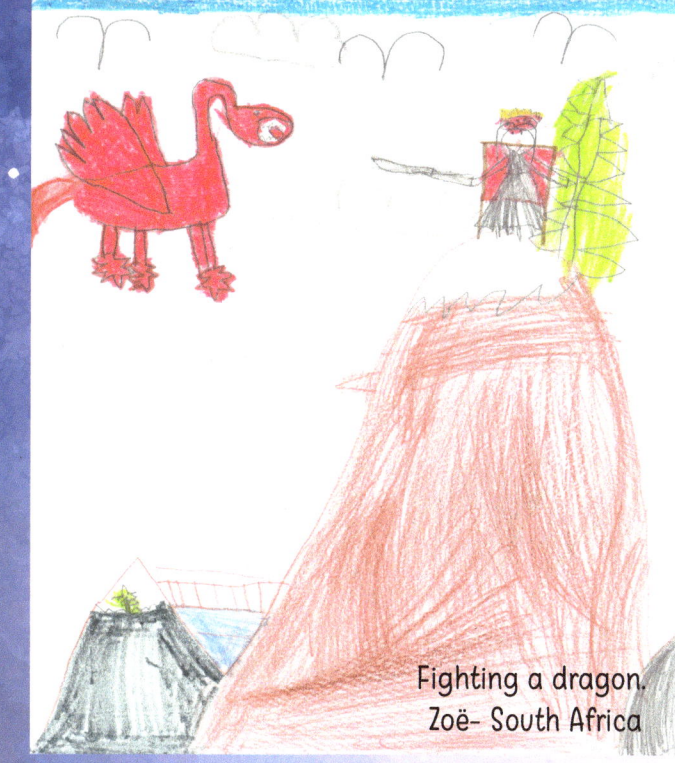

Fighting a dragon.
Zoë- South Africa

Sword of the spirit.
Naomi- Australia

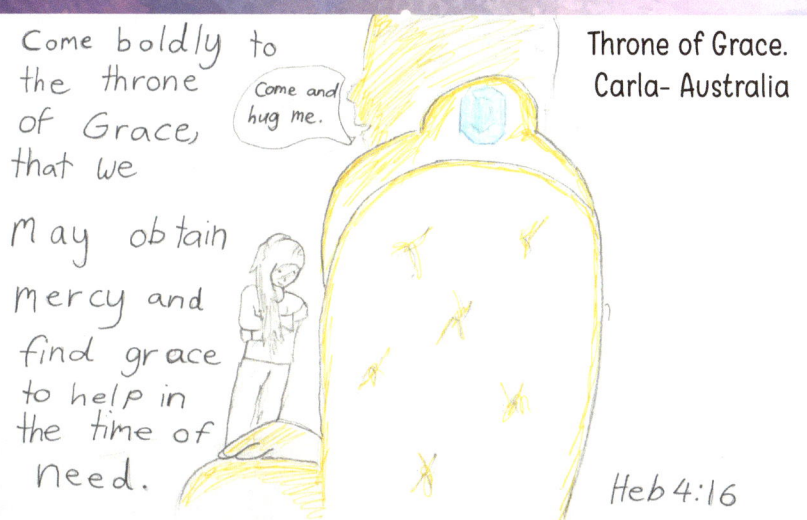

Throne of Grace.
Carla- Australia

Heb 4:16

Realms and angels.
Izak- UK

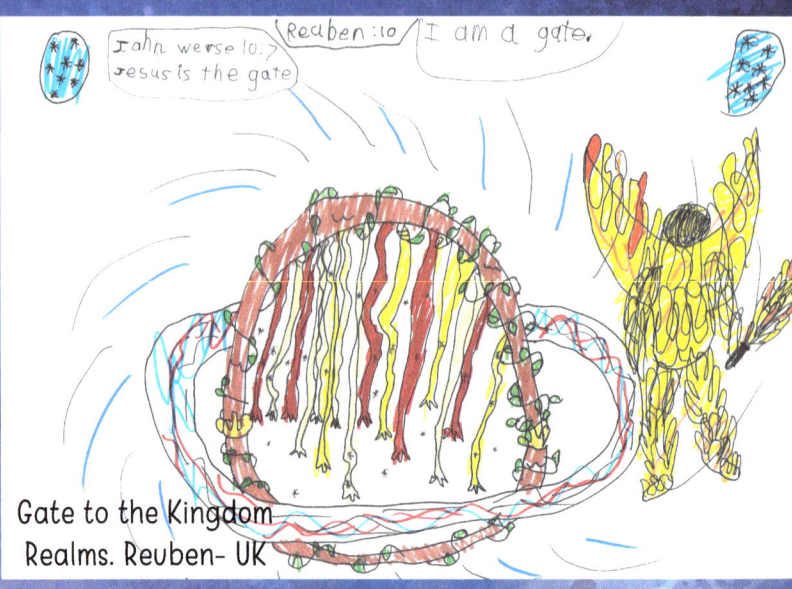

Gate to the Kingdom Realms. Reuben- UK

Sword of the Spirit.
Tatum- Australia

The Menorah.
Katie- USA

Throne of Grace.
Judah- UK

Sword of the Spirit.
Nate- South Africa

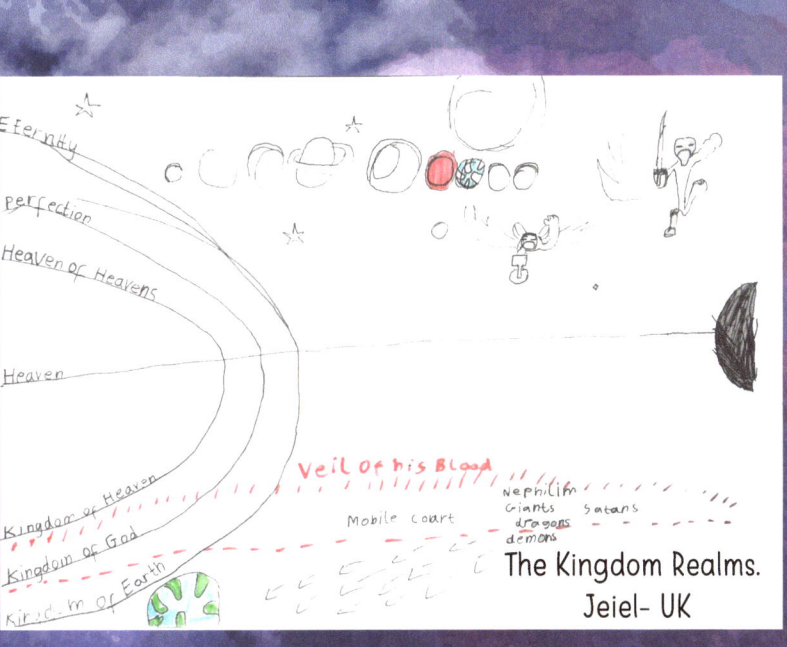

The Kingdom Realms.
Jeiel- UK

Jesus on His Throne.
Reuel- UK

www.ingramcontent.com/pod-product-compliance
Lightning Source LLC
Chambersburg PA
CBHW041154290426
44108CB00002B/69